# IMPRESSIONS *of the*
# LAKE DISTRICT

Produced by AA Publishing

© Automobile Association Developments Limited 2007

Published by AA Publishing (a trading name of Automobile Association
Developments Limited, whose registered office is Fanum House, Basing View,
Basingstoke, Hampshire RG21 4EA; registered number 1878835)

ISBN-10: 0-7495-5211-5
ISBN-13: 978-0-7495-5211-4

A03033B

A CIP catalogue record for this book is available from the British Library.

The contents of this book are believed correct at the time of printing. Nevertheless,
the publishers cannot be held responsible for any errors, omissions or for changes in
the details given in this book or for the consequences of any reliance on the
information provided by the same. This does not affect your statutory rights.

Colour reproduction by KDP, Kingsclere
Printed and bound in Thailand by Sirivatana Interprint Public Co Ltd

*Opposite: boats at Talkin Tarn in the North Pennines.*

# IMPRESSIONS *of the*
# LAKE DISTRICT

Picture Acknowledgements

The Automobile Association would like to thank the following photographers, companies
and picture libraries for their assistance in the preparation of this book.

Abbreviations for the picture credits are as follows: (AA) AA World Travel Library

3 AA/R Coulam; 5 AA/T Mackie; 7 AA/S Day; 8 AA/T Mackie; 9 AA/R Coulam; 10 AA/T Mackie; 11 AA/T
Mackie; 12 AA/T Mackie; 13 AA/R Coulam; 14 AA/T Mackie; 15 AA/S Day; 16 AA/P Sharpe; 17 AA/R Coulam;
18 AA/R Coulam; 19 AA/S Day; 20 AA/S Day; 21 AA/R Coulam; 22 AA/R Coulam; 23 AA/T Mackie; 24 AA/S
Day; 25 AA/R Coulam; 26 AA/R Coulam; 27 AA/R Coulam; 28 AA/R Coulam; 29 AA/R Coulam; 30 AA;
31 AA/P Sharpe; 32 AA/S Day; 33 AA/R Coulam; 34 AA/E A Bowness; 35 AA/T Mackie; 36 AA/T Mackie; 37 AA/E
A Bowness; 38 AA/R Coulam; 39 AA/S Day; 40 AA/T Mackie; 41 AA/E A Bowness; 42 AA/J Sparks; 43 AA/T
Mackie; 44 AA/D Tarn; 45 AA/E A Bowness; 46 AA/E A Bowness; 47 AA/E A Bowness; 48 AA/M Birkitt; 49 AA/R
Coulam; 50 AA/T Mackie; 51 AA/E A Bowness; 52 AA/P Sharpe; 53 AA/ T Mackie; 54 AA/R Coulam; 55 AA/R
Coulam; 56 AA/  Mackie; 57 AA/R Coulam; 58 AA/S Day; 59 AA/T Mackie; 60 AA/D Tarn; 61AA/R Coulam; 62
AA/E A Bowness; 63 AA/T Mackie; 64 AA/T Mackie; 65 AA/S Day; 66 AA/P Sharpe; 67 AA/J Sparks; 68 AA/S Day;
69 AA/E A Bowness; 70 AA/R Coulam; 71 AA/R Coulam; 72 AA/R Coulam; 73 AA/P Bennett; 74 AA/S Day; 75
AA/R Coulam; 76 AA/S Day; 77 AA/R Coulam; 78 AA/T Mackie; 79 AA/S Day; 80 AA/T Mackie; 81 AA/P Sharpe;
82 AA/T Mackie; 83 AA/R Coulam; 84 AA/P Sharpe; 85 AA/R Coulam; 86 AA/T Mackie; 87 AA/R Coulam; 88
AA/R Coulam; 89 AA/T Mackie; 90 AA/T Mackie; 91 AA/R Coulam; 92 AA/T Mackie; 93 AA/S Day;
94 AA/J Beazley; 95 AA/J Sparks

Every effort has been made to trace the copyright holders, and we apologise in advance for any unintentional omissions
or errors. We would be happy to apply the corrections in any following edition of this publication.

*Opposite: frosty reflections in Buttermere. The path up to Scarth Gap can be seen rising on the fell behind.*

# INTRODUCTION

The Lake District, and its surrounding county of Cumbria, occupies the far northwest corner of England. Approaching from the south its rising hills seem to bar the route of the motorway and mainline railway. Its peninsula sweeps away on the northern shore of Morecambe Bay – a line of mountains obscured by mist for much of the winter, its summits delicately tipped with snow.

But the hills are not impassable, and beyond the grey market town of Kendal, Windermere opens up with gently wooded shores and busy tourist honeypots. The hills part too to the north as the Lune Gorge gives way to the high moors around Shap and then the wide Vale of Eden. Beyond this, and beyond the great border city of Carlisle, the little-visited but no less beautiful uplands of North Cumbria merge into the Scottish Borders and Northumbrian forests.

But it is around the Lakes themselves – and the heart of the region is a National Park – that most visitors will want to linger. Grasmere and Ambleside can still take your breath away, as they did for the many poets who gathered around William Wordsworth at the beginning of the 19th century. Beatrix Potter, John Ruskin, Arthur Ransome and Alfred Wainwright were all writers who left their very different marks on the countryside they loved. Potter particularly was a champion of the Herdwick sheep, the hardy breed that is unique to these lovely fells. Ransome set his *Swallows and Amazons* on the lakes and islands of Coniston and Windermere. Wainwright brought the subtle beauty and individuality to be found in every one of the 214 fells described in his *Pictorial Guides* to an eager and loyal audience of hill walkers.

As walkers have their favourite fells (Wainwright's was reputedly Haystacks at the head of Buttermere), so many visitors also have their favourite lake. Perhaps it is Derwent Water, surrounded by distinctive peaks, or Loweswater, a quiet haven in the west. Grasmere and Rydal Water vie for the Wordsworth-inspired vote, but Ullswater has pretensions to match the finest alpine lake. Windermere is the largest, and Wast W6ater the deepest, but there are so many to see, to sit beside, or wander along a pebbly shore, that every visitor will find their own special lake.

But lakes and hills would be nothing without the valleys that connect them. Borrowdale is the dramatic haunt of climbers and walkers, and a familiar theme for pioneers of landscape art. Eskdale, way over in the west, commands an almost cult following amongst its devotees. Even getting there by car from the rest of the Lake District is hard going, requiring a hair-raising traverse of the Wrynose and Hardknott passes. The dale snakes away below you as you descend the tortuous bends beside the incredible Roman fortress. Great Langdale will always be a magnet for lovers of the dramatic – the towering peak of Harrison Stickle rising above its companion 'pikes' can be seen from all over south Lakeland.

It is impossible to do justice in a book this size to the bewildering variety to be found in the Lake District and Cumbrian countryside. But hopefully this will whet your appetite for more exploration, or serve as a reminder of this beautiful and special place.

*A golden sunset illuminates Eskdale, seen here from the Hardknott Pass.*

*Looking up to the missing chancel roof at Lanercost Priory, near Brampton. Following dissolution in 1538, the priory passed to the Dacres of nearby Naworth, who converted some of the buildings into a house. Opposite: the snowy crags of High Stile are reflected in a perfectly still Buttermere.*

*The topiary at Levens Hall. The garden is little altered since its original design in 1694 by Guillaume Beaumont, a veteran of French garden design, notably Versailles.*

*Mysterious Castlerigg stone circle near Keswick has attracted visitors since Wordsworth's days.*

*The placid lake at Ullswater is a picture of tranquillity whatever the season.*

*Blackfaced lambs are a common sight in the Border countryside in spring.*

The view over Ullswater from Hallin Fell is stunning.

Opposite: looking across Grasmere towards Dove Cottage. William Wordsworth lived here with his family from 1799 to 1808.

*The green and knotty crags of Rannerdale Knotts spill out into Crummock Water.*

*Detail from the cross at Bewcastle, which was carved from a single piece of stone in the 7th century.*

*Cricket at Lanercost. Local leagues thrive in this far-flung corner of England.*

*The Langdale Pikes form a distinctive skyline from Tarn Hows.*

*A fierce and devilish hound protects Carlisle's cathedral.*

*Opposite: looking across Borrowdale to High Spy and Narrow Moor from Surprise View, near Ashness Bridge.*

*The vaulted ceiling at Lanercost. The nave of the priory survived the trials of the dissolution to become the local parish church.*

*Clear waters below Birks Bridge, Dunnerdale. Struck by its beauty, Wordsworth composed 34 sonnets to the River Duddon.*

*Helvellyn is mirrored in the still waters of Thirlmere. The lake was extended in the 1890s to form a reservoir supplying Manchester.*

*Birdoswald's Roman fort is one of the best-preserved on Hadrian's Wall, though much of the stone was used to build the 18th-century farmhouse which overlooks the site.*

*Ivy-leaved toadflax flourishes in the stonework at Lanercost Priory.*
*Opposite: the remote borderlands beyond Bewcastle are sparsely populated. This area suffered greatly*
*in the interminable wars that raged between the Border Reivers.*

*The River Eden at Wetheral. The far bank is dominated by the ornamental cliff gardens of Corby Castle.*

*The 80ft (24m) high Wetheral Viaduct carries the Carlisle-to-Newcastle railway over the River Eden and connects the villages of Wetheral and Great Corby for pedestrians.*

*Hardknott Roman Fort, signposted from the notorious pass.*
*Opposite: the bathhouse stands outside the main wall of the fort.*

*A rainbow announces the arrival of rain off the Coniston Fells near Hawkshead.*

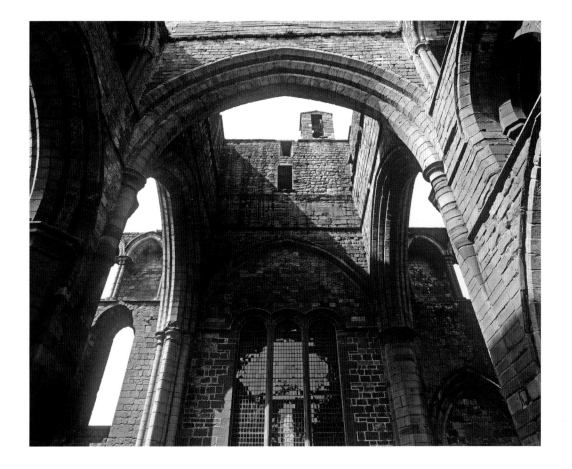

*The great arches in the tower survived Lanercost's dissolution in 1538. The priory church was restored by Anthony Salvin in the 1840s.*

*Yellow oil seed rape flowers in fields near Penrith in the Eden Valley.*

*Opposite: the Scafells and Bow Fell would have dominated the skyline for sentries on the western perimeter of Hardknott Roman Fort.*

*Cottages at Rosthwaite, Borrowdale. This busy little village is the 'capital' of the dale, with shops, campsites a youth hostel and a pub.*

*Sir William Lowther's memorial in Cartmel Priory. Holker Hall and the Cartmel estate were in Lowther hands for much of the 18th century.*

*Brantwood was the home of John Ruskin from 1872 to 1900. Overlooking Coniston Water, Brantwood is now the base for a trust conserving the work of this Victorian intellectual and artist.*

*Opposite: rowing boats line up for hire on Talkin Tarn, a glacial relic fed by underwater springs.*

*Herdwick sheep, the distinctive breed of the Lakeland fells.*

*Rowing across Grasmere. The lake was a backdrop to much of the poet Wordsworth's life.*

*From the summit of Souther Fell looking east over Greystoke Forest. In the distance are East Fellside and the North Pennines.*

*Ashness Bridge on the road to Watendlath and a much-loved view to Skiddaw.*

*Kirkby Stephen's parish church is another claimant to the title 'Cathedral of the Dales'.*
*Opposite: Harrison Stickle and the Langdale Pikes tower above Great Langdale, seen here from Elterwater.*

*Placing the capstones on a drystone wall in Great Langdale.*

*The summit of Helvellyn looms behind its Lower Man, seen across Thirlmere and a bank of Rose Bay willowherb.*

*Across Atkinson Ground to Coniston Water, a landscape inspirational to both John Ruskin and Beatrix Potter.*

*Sunlight filters through mature broadleaf woodlands at Talkin Tarn Country Park.*

*The great West Tower at Shap Abbey was completed barely 50 years before the abbey's dissolution in 1540. Opposite: a dusting of snow on the fields and fells around Windermere, seen from Orrest Head.*

*Broughton-in-Furness, a delightful old market town on the southwestern edge of the Lake District.*

*Snow caps Skiddaw on a perfectly still winter day by the shore of Derwent Water.*

*Bluebells in the graveyard of St Cuthbert's Church, Bewcastle,*
*one of Cumbria's most remote churches.*
*Opposite: sheep and their lambs on a spring evening by Talkin Tarn.*

*From Hallin Fell, Ullswater drifts away towards Dunmallard Hill and Pooley Bridge with the snow-capped North Pennines framing the horizon.*

*Arthuret church near Longtown. Some believe the parish takes its name from Rhydderch, a Celtic king and victor in a grim battle nearby, after which Merlin the wizard went mad.*

*The limestone crags of Humphrey Head point a rocky finger into Morecambe Bay.*
*Opposite: yachts moored in the evening light at Waterhead on Windermere.*

*There are seventeen major viaducts on the Settle-to-Carlisle railway. This one is at Dent Head.*

*A gravestone at Bewcastle. Legend has it that only women were buried here – the men were usually hanged and disposed of in Carlisle.*

Founded in 1123, Furness Abbey's medieval power is reflected in its massive ruins.

Opposite: an icy day on Derwent Water. The lake has frozen around Derwent Isle, and there is snow on Catbells.

*Wast Water is renowned as the deepest lake in England at 258ft (79m).*

*The bridge at Watendlath. This tiny hamlet may take its peculiar name from the Old Norse for 'the barn at the end of the lake'.*

*Wooden rowing boats line up on Keswick's lakeshore. These piers also serve the launches that ply Derwent Water.*

*Cycling on a bridleway in the Winster Valley. The Lake District's network of routes attracts cyclists from all over the world.*

*Aira Force, above Ullswater, a series of cascades criss-crossed by footbridges and cared for by the National Trust.*

*The Wordsworth family came to Rydal Mount from Grasmere in 1813 and stayed for more than forty years.*

*A well-preserved section of Hadrian's Wall in North Cumbria's World Heritage Site.*
*Opposite: the bridge over the River Esk at Longtown, not far from Gretna Green, over the Scottish border.*

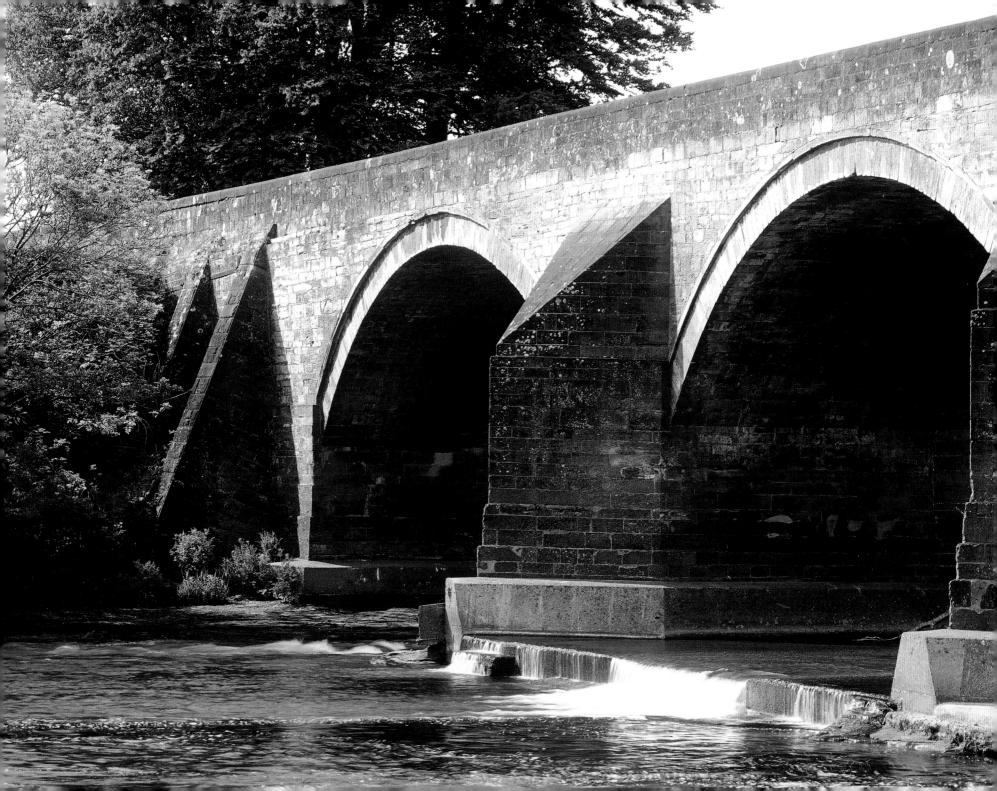

*Early moonlight casts shadows over Talkin Tarn in the North Pennines.*

*Kendal's castle ruins stand on Castle Hill. This was the home of the Parr family and birthplace of Catherine, Henry VIII's sixth and last wife.*

*The Newlands Horseshoe is a popular walk connecting Robinson (left) and Hindscarth (right).*

*A medieval preaching cross in the churchyard at Arthuret, near Longtown.
Almost nothing remains of the medieval church – it was replaced in 1609
after years of Border warfare had taken its toll.*

*An Elizabethan crest at Carlisle Cathedral. The border city was an
important English stronghold against the Scots.
Opposite: autumn colours reflect on Watendlath Tarn.*

*Looking through the topiary to Levens Hall, an Elizabethan mansion built around a medieval core.*

*A pair of swans create a ripple on Rydal Water, which for many is Cumbria's most picturesque lake.*

*The grave of the poet William Wordsworth is in Grasmere.*

*Inside the Windermere Steamboats Museum. Ten steamboats and several more motorboats are preserved from Windermere's golden age before World War I.*

*Seen from Town Cass, the snow-toppped mass of Skiddaw looms over Keswick.*

*Opposite: at Crammel Linn, near Gilsland, the River Irthing tumbles over a 30ft (10m) sandstone crag.*

*Daffodils by Ullswater. Smaller than the domestic variety, these native plants delighted Wordsworth and inspired one of his most famous poems.*

*Sheep guard the remains of Bewcastle's 13th-century castle.*

*Looking down over Ambleside from Loughrigg Fell. The town became popular with tourists and artists in Victorian times.*

*The old bridge over the Irthing at Lanercost dates from 1724.*

*Despite many changes over the years Carlisle retains some charming period shop fronts.*
*Opposite: Harrison Stickle, seen here from Great Langdale, is the highest of the Langdale Pikes.*

*Graceful High Crag forms a backdrop to the frosty shore of Buttermere.*

*The old farmhouse at Birdoswald Roman Fort is now a study centre.*

*Dove Cottage, the poet's former home, is at the heart of the Wordsworth Trust's complex at Grasmere.*

*The stone circle at Castlerigg, near Keswick, is thought to be more than 5,000 years old.*

*Devil's Bridge, Kirkby Lonsdale. The medieval structure spans the River Lune*
*in three impressive arches.*
*Opposite: looking down the length of Loweswater to Mellbreak.*

# INDEX

Aira Force 68
Ambleside 6, 86
Arthuret 57, 75
Ashness Bridge 20, 43
Atkinson Ground 48

Beaumont, Guillaume 10
Bewcastle 17, 26, 55, 61, 85
Birdoswald 25, 91
Birks Bridge 23
boats 38, 41, 58, 63, 66, 81
Border Reivers 27
Borrowdale 6, 20, 36
Bow Fell 35
Brantwood 39
bridges 43, 65, 71, 87, 94
Broughton-in-Furness 52
Buttermere 5, 6, 8, 90

Carlisle 6, 21, 77, 88
Carlisle-to-Newcastle railway 29
Cartmel Priory 37
Castlerigg stone circle 11, 93
castles 73, 85
Catbells 63
cathedrals 21, 77
churches 22, 33, 44, 55, 57, 61, 75
crosses, stone 17, 75
Coniston Fells 32
Coniston Water 6, 39, 48
Corby Castle 28
Crammel Linn 83
Crummock Water 16
cycling 67

Dacre family 9
Dent Head 60
Derwent Water 6, 53, 63, 66
Devil's Bridge 94

Dove Cottage, Grasmere 15, 92
drystone walls 46
Duddon, River 23
Dunmallard Hill 56
Dunnerdale 23

East Fellside 42
Eden, River 28, 29
Eden Valley 6, 34
Elterwater 45
Esk, River 71
Eskdale 6, 7

Furness Abbey 62

Grasmere 6, 15, 41, 80, 92
Great Langdale 6, 45, 46, 89
Greystoke Forest 42

Hadrian's Wall 25, 70
Hallin Fell 14, 56
Hardknott Pass 6, 7
Hardnott Roman fort 6, 30–1, 35
Harrison Stickle 6, 45, 89
Hawkshead 32
Haystacks 6
Helvellyn 24, 47
Herdwick sheep 40
High Crag 90
High Spy 20
High Stile 8
Hindscarth 74
Holker Hall 37
Humphrey Head 59

Irthing, River 83, 87

Kendal 6, 73

Keswick 66, 82
Kirkby Lonsdale 94
Kirkby Stephen 44

Lanercost 18, 87
Lanercost Priory 9, 22, 27, 33
Langdale Pikes 19, 45, 89
Levens Hall 10, 78
Longtown 57, 71
Loughrigg Fell 86
Lower Man 47
Loweswater 6, 95
Lowther, Sir William 37
Lune, River 94
Lune Gorge 6

Mellbreak 95
Merlin 57
Morecambe Bay 6, 59

Narrow Moor 20
Newlands Horseshoe 74

Orrest Head 50

Parr, Catherine 73
Pennines 42, 56, 72
Penrith 34
Pooley Bridge 56
Potter, Beatrix 6, 48

Rannerdale Knotts 16
Ransome, Arthur 6
Rhydderch 57
Robinson 74
Roman remains 6, 25, 30–1, 35, 70
Rosthwaite 36
Ruskin, John 6, 39, 48
Rydal Mount 69

Rydal Water 6, 79

Salvin, Anthony 33
Scafells 35
Scarth Gap 5
Settle-Carlisle railway 60
Shap 6
Shap Abbey 51
sheep 13, 40, 54, 85
Skiddaw 43, 53, 82
Souther Fell 42
stone circle, Castlerigg 11, 93
Surprise View 20

Talkin Tarn 38, 49, 54, 72
Tarn Hows 19
Thirlmere 2, 47
topiary 10, 78

Ullswater 6, 12, 14, 56, 68, 84

viaducts 29, 60

Wainwright, Alfred 6
walls, drystone 46
Wast Water 6, 64
Watendlath 43, 65
Watendlath Tarn 76
waterfalls 68, 83
Waterhead 58
Wetheral 28
Wetheral Viaduct 29
Windermere 6, 50, 58
Windermere Steamboats Museum 81
Winster Valley 67
Wordsworth, William 6, 14, 23, 41, 69, 80, 84, 92
Wrynose Pass 6